Mount Rushmore

Lori Dittmer

Creative Education · Creative Paperbacks

Road map of
Contents

Black Hills
South Dakota

Welcome to Mount Rushmore! This **sculpture** features the faces of four presidents. It is part of Mount Rushmore National **Memorial** in South Dakota's Black Hills.

George Washington is on the far left. Beside him are Thomas Jefferson, Theodore Roosevelt, and Abraham Lincoln. Each person represents an important time in United States history.

USA
Mount Rushmore faces
about 60 feet (18.3 m)

Brazil
Christ the Redeemer
125 feet (38.1 m)

Egypt
Great Sphinx of Giza
66 feet (20.1 m)

How tall are the Mount Rushmore carvings?

U.K.
Stonehenge
30 feet (9.1 m)

school bus
10.5 feet (3.2 m)

adult human
6 feet (1.8 m)

A South Dakota man thought someone should carve historical figures into the Black Hills. Gutzon Borglum got the job. He wanted the sculpture to be for the whole country. He picked four presidents.

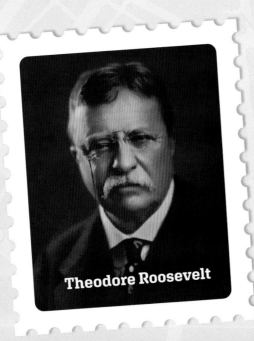

Theodore Roosevelt

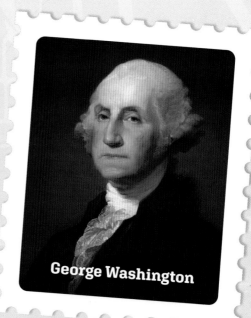

George Washington

Can you match each president's picture to his stone face above?

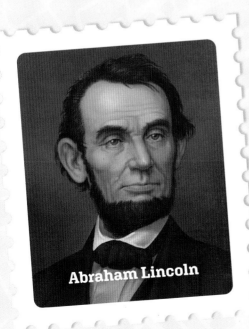

Abraham Lincoln

Thomas Jefferson

Borglum (pictured) chose Mount Rushmore for its hard granite. He also liked the way the morning sun lit the area. First, he made a scale model. The actual **monument** is 12 times bigger. Carving began in 1927. It was finished in 1941.

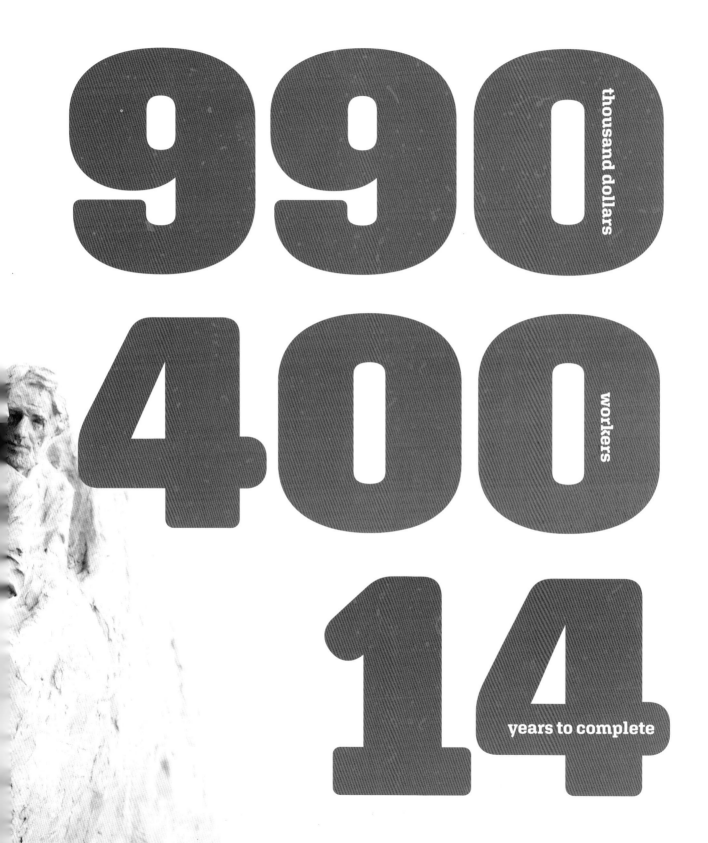

990 thousand dollars

400 workers

14 years to complete

Workers did 90 percent of the carving with dynamite . More than 450,000 tons (408,233 t) of rock fell down the mountainside. Then workers sat in bosun's chairs . They were lowered into place on cables. They shaped the stone with jackhammers and drills. Finally, they made each 60-foot (18.3 m) face smooth.

Borglum sealed cracks with a linseed oil mixture. Today, workers use stronger materials. They watch for large cracks. They make sure the rock does not move.

Nearly 3 million people visit Mount Rushmore each year. If you go, visit the Sculptor's Studio. Borglum worked on his model there. Follow the Presidential Trail for a closer view of the faces. At night, watch the lighting ceremony from the **amphitheater**.

Nearby, another carved face gazes across the landscape. You can visit the Lakota warrior Chief Crazy Horse Memorial. This is still a work in progress.

under construction since 1948 - **CRAZY HORSE MEMORIAL** - will be nearly 10 times the size of Mount Rushmore when complete

Scaling Up

pen or pencil   **grid paper**

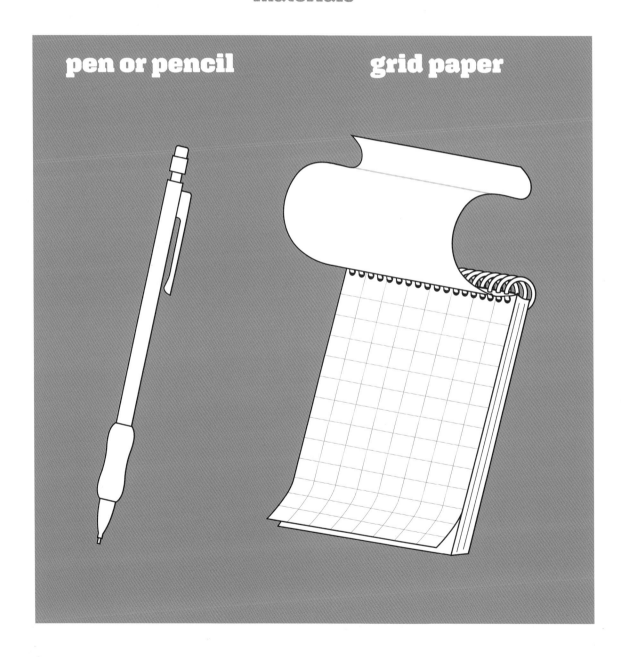

On one sheet of paper, draw a rectangle. Use the grid squares as a guide.

Next, draw a rectangle that is two times larger than the first. Be sure to double the length and height of the first rectangle.

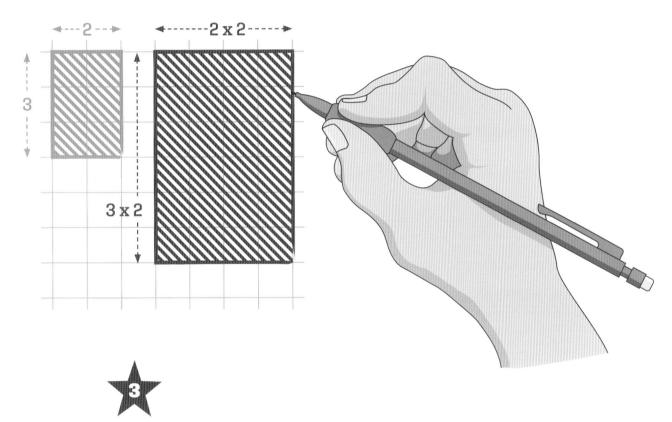

Can you make the shape four times bigger? Gutzon Borglum scaled his models 12 times bigger. Can you scale up other shapes?

Glossary

★ amphitheater ★

a large, open area surrounded by tiered rows of seats

★ bosun's chairs ★

devices used to hold people in the air as they work

★ dynamite ★

a type of explosive

★ memorial ★

something that reminds people of a person or event

★ monument ★

a structure built to honor a person or event

★ sculpture ★

artwork that is two- or three-dimensional,
so it can be seen from different sides

Read More

Chang, Kirsten. *Mount Rushmore*. Minneapolis: Bellwether Media, 2019.

Conley, Kate. *Engineering Mount Rushmore*. Minneapolis: Abdo, 2018.

Websites

National Park Service: Mount Rushmore National Memorial
Learn more about the history of Mount Rushmore and the presidents featured on it.

https://www.nps.gov/moru/index.htm

YouTube: The History of Mount Rushmore for Kids: Famous Landmarks for Children
Watch a video about the history of Mount Rushmore.

https://www.youtube.com/watch?v=fApIefqUvSo

Note: Every effort has been made to ensure that the websites listed above are suitable for children, that they have educational value, and that they contain no inappropriate material. However, because of the nature of the Internet, it is impossible to guarantee that these sites will remain active indefinitely or that their contents will not be altered.

Index

**PUBLISHED BY CREATIVE EDUCATION
AND CREATIVE PAPERBACKS**
P.O. Box 227, Mankato, Minnesota 56002
Creative Education and Creative Paperbacks
are imprints of The Creative Company
www.thecreativecompany.us

**LIBRARY OF CONGRESS CATALOGING-
IN-PUBLICATION DATA**
Names: Dittmer, Lori, author.
Title: Mount Rushmore / Lori Dittmer.
Series: Landmarks of America.
Includes bibliographical references and index.
Summary: Examining the building process
from the ground up, this high-interest title
covers the history and construction of
Mount Rushmore, one of South Dakota's
most well-known landmarks.

Identifiers: LCCN: 2018061069
ISBN 978-1-64026-127-3 (hardcover)
ISBN 978-1-62832-690-1 (pbk)
ISBN 978-1-64000-245-6 (eBook)

Subjects: LCSH: Mount Rushmore National
Memorial (S.D.)—Juvenile literature.
Classification: LCC F657.R8 D58 2019
DDC 978.3/93—dc23

DESIGN AND PRODUCTION
by Joe Kahnke; art direction by Rita Marshall
Printed in China

PHOTOGRAPHS by Alamy (Everett
Collection Historical, ibrandify, Tribune
Content Agency LLC, Wiskerke), Creative
Commons Wikimedia (Strobridge & Co.
Lith., printer/Library of Congress, Gilbert
Stuart/Clark Art Institute), Getty Images
(Bettmann, Pawel Gaul, George Rinhart/
Corbis Historical), iStockphoto (Leontura),
Shutterstock (aarrows, BATKA, dikobraziy,
Dr_Flash, Jess Kraft, Rainer Lesniewski,
Jennifer O'Connor, Jim Parkin, John Parrot/
Stocktrek Images)

FIRST EDITION HC 9 8 7 6 5 4 3 2 1
FIRST EDITION PBK 9 8 7 6 5 4 3 2 1